IN WILDERNESS
Song
Litany of the Common Loon

Stephen Kirkpatrick

"*Of all the wild creatures which still persist in the land, despite settlement and civilization, the loon seems best to typify the untamed savagery of the wilderness.*"

Edward Howe Forbush, 1912

IN WILDERNESS

Litany of the Common Loon

Published by:

Thy Marvelous Works

P.O. Box 31414
Jackson, MS 39286

First Edition

Printed & bound by:
Quebecor Printing
Kingsport, TN

Color Separations by:
K & W Prepress
Jackson, MS

Designed by:
Sam Beibers

Text edited by:
Ann Becker

Jacket design by:
Jennifer Hydrick

Library of Congress Catalog
95-94050

ISBN # 0-9619353-8-3

Dedication

To my sons Sean, Ryan & Ian
May you always seek not only to know but also to understand.

Acknowledgements

It is always an impossible task to give heartfelt thanks to those who directly contribute to the completion of difficult endeavors such as a book. There are always those whose care with such matters need special recognition. I know that your contributions are from love and trust in myself. That carries a heavy weight of responsibility. I pray I never lose that trust. Thank you from my heart.

Mr. O. L. Kirkpatrick - the giver of Half Crown and its loons
Julia Jervis - tender words of enthusiasm
Susan Kirkpatrick - sibling strength
Penny Hoz - a mother's love
Ted Hoz - foundational support
Amelia Gamblin - calm in my season of discontent
Bobby McCain - a friend indeed
Sam Beibers - humble creativity
Ann Becker - prose doctor
Tommy Lynch & Charlie Dyar - truly photos plus

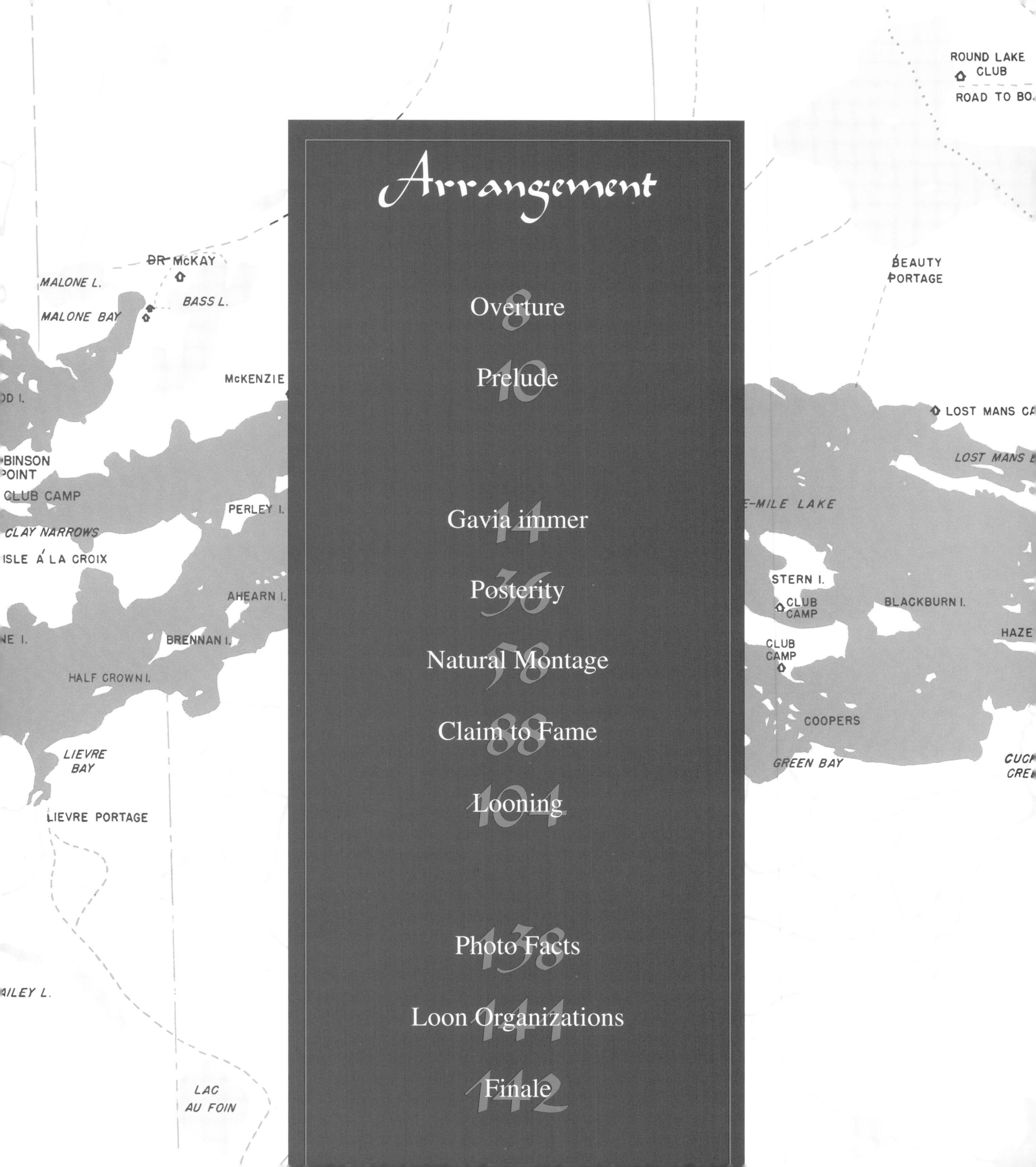

Arrangement

Overture

" *Among the picturesque lakes of wilder, wooded portions of the northern states and Canada - where dark firs and spruces mingle with graceful white birches, cast their reflections in the still, clear waters - sportsmen and appreciative nature lovers have found attractive summer resorts. Here, far from the cares of the busy world, one finds true recreation in his pursuit of speckled trout, real rest in his camp among the fragrant balsams, and genuine joy in his communion with nature in her wildest solitudes. The woodland lake would be solitudes, indeed, did they lack the finishing touch to make the picture complete, the tinge of wildness which adds color to the scene, the weird and mournful cry of the loon, as he calls to his mate or greets some new arrival. Who has ever paddled a canoe, or cast a fly, or pitched a tent in the north woods and has not stopped to listen to this wail of the wilderness? And what would the wilderness be without it?"*

Arthur Cleveland Bent, 1919

Prelude

"Today I had my first encounter with the common loon. My immediate reaction to this remarkable creature was that there is nothing 'common' about it at all. I was visually stimulated by the black-and-white feather patterns and the red eyes. A silky iridescence causes the coal-black feathers of the head and neck to turn shades of forest green.

"Last night was the first calm, quiet night on the lake. My sleep was restless for I played audience to a huge stage. What I had mistaken as the mournful calls of wolves and coyotes turned out to be the cries of the loon!

"Outside my cabin window now I can hear the lapping rhythm of waves upon the rocks. A cool breeze is breathing in. Varying nuances of sound are drifting about with differing emphasis of melody. I am entranced by all of this. I have awakened a new sensitivity to sound within myself. I look forward now, night after night, to the rhapsody in the wilderness. I'm hooked.

"This world in which the loon lives is idyllic. Its summer sojourn to raise its young and feed in these ever-clear waters is a natural. Recording a description here seems impossible. Cool nights, beautiful flowers, bird songs, puffy white clouds, howling wolves - all this is part of the stimulation for my craft. The sunrises and sunsets are wonders enough, but then mix in full moons, morning fog and misty rain and...well, I must lay down my pen and write with light on film.

"Tonight I find myself thinking about my Southern swamps. They have always called to my heart. They are equally enchanting as this Northern retreat, but this haunting wilderness is all new to me. Through this short-lived, uniquely summer experience some 1,700 miles from my Mississippi home, I'm experiencing the song of the North country, which is music to my ears and my eyes."

August 1979

"*I* can remember those feelings I wrote in my journal some fifteen years ago as if it were yesterday. Such experiences summer after summer birthed the idea of a loon book back in 1983. Over the years I have kept notes on behavior and photographic experiences while putting in time observing these wonderful birds. I have also kept a scrapbook (a scrapbox really) of things I have heard and read about loons that I thought interesting, and I've penned memories and thoughts. What is offered here is a journal of sorts, the life times of the north woods.

"As I sit writing and sketching, it is a blustery day here in Quebec. The loons are quiet for now, but at any moment their calls could ring out and again I will be reminded that on these Northern waters swims not only a bird so unusual it demands attention, but also a sojourn of my own that becomes ever more necessary to my well being. Without it the celebration of wilderness is not complete. This experience is not known by all, but by all who have known it, it is not forgotten."

July 1994

Gavia immer

"With the exception of that most expert of all Divers, the Anhinga and the Great Auk, the loon is perhaps the most accomplished. Whether it be fishing in deep water amid rolling billows, or engaged in eluding its foes, it disappears beneath the surface so suddenly, remains so long in the water, and rises at so extraordinary a distance, often in a direction quite the reverse of that supposed to be followed by it, that your eyes become wearied in searching for it, and you renounce the wish of procuring it out of sheer vexation....I felt as if I could not have pulled my oars any longer, and was willing to admit that I was outdone by a loon."

John James Audubon, 1840

Gavia immer: the word "gavia" is Latin for "sea mew." The word "immer" is also Latin, derived from "immergo" or "immersus," which mean to immerse or submerge.

The word "immer" also could be old Swedish, English or Norwegian in derivation. The Swedish "emmer" (ashen or black), the English "hymber" (ashen or black) or the Norwegian "hymber," meaning "embergoose," all are descriptive of the loon.

The word "loon" can be traced back to several sources. "Loom," which is a Shetland name for the bird, is Scandinavian for "diving bird" or "water bird." It could also come from a Scandinavian word "lumme" which means "lummox" or "clumsy." This could refer to the loon's inability to move well on land. The best description I have found is that of an old Norse word, "lomr." This captures the essence of the loon perfectly. It means "lament" or "wail."

The Common Loon (*Gavia immer*) is the first species of the first family of U.S. birds. There are 4 other species of loons:

- Arctic Loon (*Gavia arctica*)
- Red-throated Loon (*Gavia stellata*), the smallest loon
- Pacific Loon (Gavia pacifica)
- Yellow-billed Loon (*Gavia adamsii*), the largest loon

The Yellow-billed Loon is the most similar to the Common Loon, sharing exact coloration. The only difference is in the bill of the larger bird, which is ivory-colored and slightly upturned. The Common Loon has a black bill. The Yellow-billed Loon is also the least likely to be seen by birders, since it spends most of its life in the far reaches of the Arctic, breeding in northern Russia, across Alaska and northern Canada. It is most abundant along the Arctic coast and eastern Siberia.

The Common Loon breeds in the extreme northern U.S. and Alaska, Canada, Greenland and Iceland. It is often recorded in its summer, nuptial plumage in Florida, Georgia, Alabama, Mississippi, Louisiana and Texas. There has been no account of breeding activity in any of these sightings. Most likely these are immature birds not yet in the breeding cycle.

Loons comprise a distinctive group of Holarctic birds. They show a very high degree of specialization to aquatic life. Other than in the summer breeding season, their habitat is essentially a maritime one, particularly estuaries and inshore waters in the Northern Hemisphere only.

Albinism, even though rarely seen, has been recorded. The loon is also a protected bird under the l918 "Migratory Bird Treaty Act."

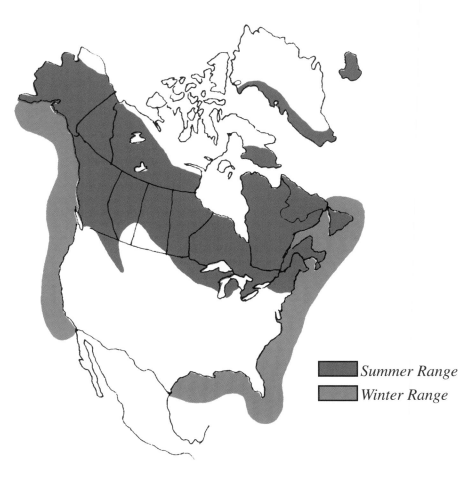

■ *Summer Range*
■ *Winter Range*

" *L*oons are often playful, comical, almost silly birds. At the same time they have an elegance seen nowhere else in the animal kingdom. This is evident even at first glance. They appear to be sporting fine tuxedos. They even have a feathered necklace & flaunt rubies for eyes! "

1983

" *I* watched a loon swim beneath my boat today. Never once did it use its wings for propulsion, although it would make sense that in a sharp turn they may become useful and forsake their tight, aerodynamic tuck. "

1982

The loon can reach an underwater speed of 30 miles per hour for short distances. They have also been recorded at 200 feet below the water's surface. An average dive seems to be around a minute, although they can stay under about three minutes if necessary. Their torpedo-like torso with nearly solid, heavy bones helps in their aquatic pursuits. Their feet, at the extreme rear of their bodies, are used alternately "oar fashion" except for when a short burst of speed is needed and a "simultaneous stroke" is used. Some people are of the opinion that loons can stay for extended periods underwater. This misconception can be explained by their unpredictable surfacing and their ability to dive without surfacing, only raising head and nostrils above the water's surface for a full breath of air.

Fish comprise 90% of the loon's diet, although crayfish, leeches, large insects, frogs, crustaceans and an array of vegetable matter will suffice. Fish are almost always eaten underwater, although I have witnessed a large fish brought to the surface and eaten. They also 'grab' as opposed to 'spear.' Eating 'trash' fish and slow or weak 'game' fish, loons offer no competition to fishermen.

Taking to the air is no easy chore for the loon. Running into a head wind for at least 50 yards is needed. A quarter mile may be needed at other times! Once in the air they are swift fliers, around 70 mph., needfully so. If their flight was slowed down too much, they would come out of the air like bricks.

"*I've noticed this arched body 'gliding' from time to time. I see it more in late summer and fall, but not often in either case.*"

1988

Even though no "rafting" is done, as ducks do, rich vocalizations & large gatherings can be witnessed before leaving for warmer waters. Too late an exodus could leave loons trapped by ice with no space for their long take off.

Migration is "high & silent" in scattered flocks of 6 to 60, apparently taking no notice of each other.

"*Today, Dick Weber, chairman of the North America Loon Fund, and I were checking some unusual loon nesting sights. While we were out he told me about a pair of loons which were found a couple of years ago that were "iced in" on a nearby lake. A local observer managed to catch them and Delta Air Lines flew them down to Florida. I hope they don't let the others know about this 'easy' migration. Imagine Delta with a half-million loons on board. They would have to have plenty of 'fish snacks!'*"

1994

"*Watching a loon land is interesting. Needing a somewhat shallow glide, they more or less 'crash land,' sometimes with a big bounce or two, albeit with a touch of grace on calm water.*"

1991

" I learned first hand about the aggressive nature of an angry loon. They have been recorded attacking raccoons, foxes and even polar bears! Their large, sharp bill is their weapon. I read of a photographer trying to photograph loons underwater being attacked and struck right above the mask, drawing blood and leaving a vivid memory of loon aggression. "

1987

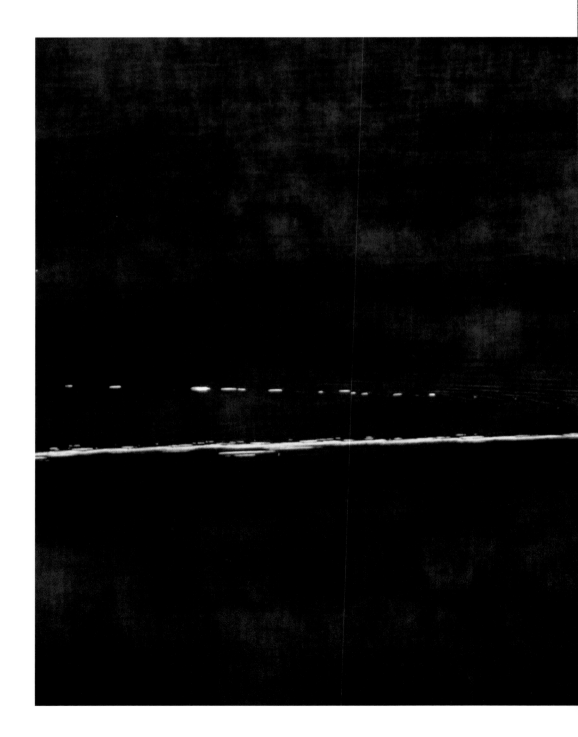

love watching the loons in their element. They seemingly glide over the surface of an isolated cove or calm lake. I wonder sometimes if the water escapes agitation altogether. Suddenly they submerge their eyes beneath the surface to survey the depths below. Soon they dive; with absolute grace they abandon their preening and oiling to feed below. Their lightning speed and inherent skills underwater propel their reputation as master fishermen. Minutes later, with quarry safely put away, they return to the surface to continue adorning the natural world."

1986

"*A* young loon attempted to eat a fresh-water clam, by inserting its bill into the open shell of the mollusk, which was about 2 inches long; the young loon found the clam too strong for it and lost part of its bill in consequence."

W. F. Ganong, 1890

*"*W*inter birds are solitary. I have witnessed them by the hundreds on the Gulf of Mexico and Atlantic coasts. Their molt at that time of year leaves them a dull gray-brown. They are also silent for the most part. With the coming of spring their beautiful plumage is back as well as their enriching song. Breeding & courtship behavior are very subtle but noticeable. They seem to have an unusual way about them. Bill dipping with cocked necks and soft cooing is about the extent of this quiet nuptial bliss.*"*

1994

"$\mathcal{T}$he cramped quarters of my blind made getting into different positions nearly impossible. As the loon climbed onto her nest, my angle of view was perfect to see her legs, observing the awkwardness of an earthbound loon. This very fact is what makes them masters of the depths!"

1994

"The pollen has been unbelievable. On calm days the surface of the water is as covered with debris as my watery eyes!"

1994

"*The breeze has been refreshing today. From time to time the solitude has called to me. Nesting is in its last stages and most of the loon world is quiet. I did see one pair whose loonlings obviously did not make it. Eggshells but no chicks – could have been Herring Gulls or maybe pike.*"

1994

This seeker of solitude has low reproduction potential. A pair of loons average one surviving chick every 3 or 4 years. Lakes with islands are highest in reproduction percentages. In these, predators on eggs, (raccoons being the worst), are at a minimum. The job of keeping a loonling alive after hatching is a real challenge. Herring Gulls, snapping turtles, ravens & Northern Pike are all constant threats. If an egg is lost, loons may re-nest; if a chick is lost they will not. Carrying a chick on the back is one way the loon can reduce the chance of a chick being attacked.

"Today we conducted the North American Loon Count...it was a success, 87 loons and 15 young were turned in from the area."

July 17, 1994

"So far 9 nests have been located and monitored. Results as follows:

1. 2 eggs, 0 chicks

2. 2 eggs, 2 chicks

3. 2 eggs, 1 chick

4. 3 eggs, 0 chicks (nested twice same place)

5. 2 eggs, not hatched

6. 2 eggs, 1 chick

7. 2 eggs, not hatched (a re-nest, different location)

8. 2 eggs, 2 chicks

9. 2 eggs, not hatched (same nest and loons as #8, do not understand)"

July 28, 1994

" *C*hicks witness and experience behavior they will use the rest of their lives. The 'crippled loon' act & 'penguin dancing' are tactical ploys to distract possible intruders while chicks head for safety. My observations seem to show the female doing more of these tactics while the male often stays closer to the young. However, these antics are often done simultaneously. Immature birds, often in groups, can be seen 'practicing' these maneuvers. It appears as a circus. I believe they also do this as a means of building up stamina for the soon-to-be-undertaken experience of migration. "

1990

"What a sight! While shooting a pair of loons with their two-week-old young, a single loon sailed quietly overhead. It turned and landed nearby. The early morning light added drama to the next few minutes as the pair took up defense postures and the male yodeled constantly. The unwelcome loon seemed to 'not get it' and he just hung around until the chick headed for safety. Both parents got very aggressive and surrounded the intruder. Never did they do anything that would suggest 'attack.' The intruder soon left and took to the skies. What an experience!"

1992

"*Today I discovered loons are fearless defenders of their young & territory. I approached too close to a young loonling and found myself facing the flaring throat and resounding voice of a very angry male loon. His tensed, open mouth got frightfully close to my face. I flinched and fell back in horror. The loon dove and immediately returned to the young chick while I lay in the bottom of the boat. I felt horrible; I didn't mean to upset them. I also have never been confronted before by their large size & aggressive manner. I've acquired a new love, respect and concern for the loon.*"

1982

" *Between two and four weeks old, the young loon is not really black or brown.* "

1983

"*I found today some six-week-old loons. This would mean nothing if it weren't the first week of October! Even the adult was molting into winter plumage.*"

1994

"Observing these beautiful divers for hours is no chore. They simply enhance all existence with their seemingly continuous song. Their careful attention to their young and neverending quest for food transform the hours into minutes and my time is preserved in beautiful memories."

1988

Natural Montage

"...Formerly, when lying awake at midnight in those woods, I had listened to hear some words or syllables of their language, but it chanced that I listened in vain until I heard the cry of the loon. I have heard it occasionally on the ponds of my native town, but there its wildness is not enhanced by the surrounding scenery.

I was awakened at midnight by some heavy, low-flying bird, probably a loon, flapping by close over my head, along the shore. So, turning the other side of my half-clad body to the fire, I sought slumber again."

Henry David Thoreau

July 27, 1857

"In my youth I remember seeing Indian Pipes during summer camp in the hills of North Carolina and thought they were mushrooms. Today I shot a photogenic group of them on the south slope of the Big Loge near my 'loon lookout.' Conditions must be right, because I saw quite few of these unique flowers."

1992

"Great day! Trillium, bellwort, bullfrog, robins, waterfalls, ferns, ruddy turnstones, loons in fog, clintonia and fringed polygala. My senses are on fire!"

1994

"*I think today I might have finally caught the leaves motionless over the stream. The constant wind and air turbulence has made this a frustrating shot to get for 2 weeks! The 4 & 8-second exposures needed to contrast movement with stillness are frustrating me, but it might have happened today. The overflowing beaver pond is running down into a nearby cove where I constantly see a pair of loons. They are obviously not nesting. I wonder if they enjoy the beautiful falls or love the sound of rushing water as much as I do?*"

1994

"*The streams are filled with naiads of dragonflies and damselflies. I found myself cheering them on as insects welted my skin. I was in need of some natural predators for relief! There is a species of blackfly that only attacks loons; I'm sure the loons were rooting, too.*"

1994

"There have been a lot of mergansers on the lake lately. While photographing one recently it passed right in front of a Pink Lady's Slipper Orchid growing close to the water's edge. What a sight! Yesterday someone reported to me they had seen a 'strange-looking loon' on the lake. The merganser, I'm sure, was flattered."

1994

"*While I was searching the shoreline for columbine, an inquisitive mink popped his head up out of a piece of driftwood. He seemed to look at me as if to ask 'what do you want?' He ran back and forth among the wood & rocks, capturing my attention and frustrating my focusing finger at every frame.*"

1994

"*The blue flag iris are profuse! Their quiet lavender petals and yellow throats add a splash of color to the landscape, especially around the sensitive & cinnamon ferns growing thick around the beaver ponds.*"

1994

"Pale Corydalis has enhanced the rocky islands with pink and yellow flowers. One bunch has dressed up a nearby loon nest."

1994

"The blustery day with puffy white clouds was a classic. The pair of loons I have been watching on 'gull island' have successfully hatched 1 chick. It is incredible that they nested so near some 150 gulls. A few gull nests are only 8 feet from their nest. Nearly all are Ring-billed Gulls, maybe this is why."

1994

"*Paddling through Lievre Bay today I was gently and slowly moving through bullhead lilies when I noticed a light pattern in the rushes to my right. There, perfectly still, was an American Bittern. My camera was not in easy reach in the shaky canoe. The lilies held me in place as I held my breath and steadied for 4 shots before a squawking departure was observed. What a find!*"

1991

"*The sunrise was absolutely wonderful this morning. The fog was thick but seemed to dissipate at the right moments as the sun broke over the distant hills. The ghostly images of trees on the isolated rocks added wonderful structure to the mood. I imagine loons have seen this scene many times when my eyes have not yet opened to this wonderful time of the day.*"

1994

"*Today while working near Beauty Lake I spotted some sundew growing on an old beaver lodge. As I positioned myself, careful not to disturb the scene, a bullfrog appeared before my eyes in the midst of the carnivorous plants. The reds & greens were electrifying!*"

1991

"*Last night a lightning storm moved through about 9 p.m. It lasted nearly two hours! I got to shoot for about an hour before the rain was too much. I think I got some multiple lightning shots over the far hills. Several times it appeared as if the Big Loge summit took some direct hits. All evening and on through the night the loons were totally silent.*"

1994

"*It was incredible, the Black Duck just stayed there preening! A breeze came up and blew the front of the canoe towards him and he was gone. I'm somewhat concerned about the image as I was shooting with a 400mm lens at 1/30 of a second, hand held from the shaky canoe. I'm thinking that the shots may not come out.*"

1992

Summer
1994

May 30 Snappy turtle on dam, Pale Corydalis, loons (water level : sunset), nesting gulls merganser in flight
31 waterfalls, loon in flight, squirrel, garter snake, starflower, Jack in pulpit
~~June 1~~ mushrooms, flowers (Rose Twisted-Stalk, Clintonia) Red Trillium, loons

June 1 Loons (flight, nest, sunrise), waterfalls, robins, fringed Polygala
mallards + B. ducks, dragonfly, redbelt? (mushroom)

June 2 Trillium, Clintonia, Large-Flowered Bellwort, Frog, Robins, Waterfalls (Lower)
Ruddy Turnstone ✔, Ferns

June 3 Robins, loons, fog at sunrise, grebe?, mink, turtles, sunset
gulls, mergansers, columbine, frog, shadbush, scenery

June 4 Columbine, Shadbush, Gulls, reflections, Ruddy Turnstone
Hummingbird, Robins, loons, marsh marigolds, brown lake creek, loons
air plane + water, Phoebe, Song Sparrow, sunset, beaver

June 5 Sunrise, in Loring Bay, gulls at sunrise, waterfalls, robins, song sparrow, shadbush
sunset, gulls, loons, mergansers

June 6 loons in rain + yodel, merganser

June 7 loons, Black duck at nest, song sparrow eggs, pink lady's slipper,
salamander (dusky), columbine, sunset

June 8 Bunchberry, violets, ferns, (mayfly, dragonfly, crane flies all
in dew) fringed Polygala, Jack-in-pulpit (group), pink lady slipper,
Banded water snake, merganser, scenery, Ferns

June 9 Loons + nest, yellow lady slipper, Gulls in flight, pink lady slipper

June 10 Loons in fog, dragonfly + moth in dew, great Blue early, loons, beaver

June 11 loons, sunrise + gulls, song sparrow + nest,

June 12 _____ what's the name of that lake?

June 13 Song Sparrow + nest, Loon at nest, banded water snake

June 14 loons in fog, leopard frog(?), bluet + violet, flower (?), Ferns,
damselfly, stream, Purple Avens

June 15 Loons on nest!

"*This evening I saw the strangest sight. I was setting up at sunset and was watching the bats satiate their appetites on insects when from my left a Sharp-shinned Hawk zips by, nailing a bat with a 'thump.' His flight was not altered or slowed in the least.*"

1994

"*Each night we sat there looking down the waterway, listening to the loons filling the darkening narrows with wild reverberating music but it was when they stopped that the quiet descended, an all-pervading stillness that absorbed all the sounds that had ever been. No one spoke. We sat there so removed from the rest of the world and with such a sense of complete remoteness that any sound would have been a sacrilege.*"

Sigurd F. Olson, 1938

Basically four sounds are the source for all loon communication. The wail, tremolo, yodel & hoot.

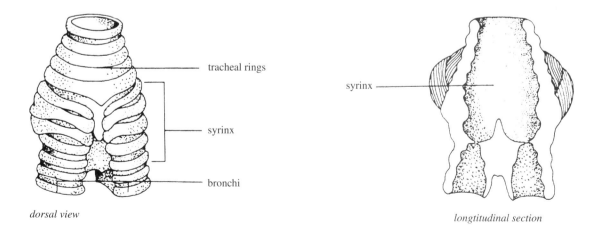

tracheal rings

syrinx

bronchi

dorsal view

syrinx

longtitudinal section

After all is said and read, there is really only one thing that endures in the human soul about the loon, and that is their song. It is at the same time intriguing, disturbing and soothing. Its uniqueness is the communicative quality employing only a few sounds. Unique not only to the loon, but also to nearly all birds is the syrinx. Sounds are created by a vibrating membrane in this bony, boxlike chamber. Birds have a larynx but no vocal chords. The larynx is used to regulate the air flow between the pharynx and trachea. The syrinx is located at the lower end of the trachea, affording a long, resonating chamber for their peerless song.

The wail is a long, moaning call made by the flexing of the throat. It is much like the howls of coyotes & wolves. A soothing sound I label the 'where are you?' call. It has three basic variations:

        1) a single, drawn-out note

        2) a single note with a second drawn out note higher in pitch

        3) the same as the second variation with a third note, either higher or lower in pitch.

The tremolo is a short, wavering sound made by the rapid opening and closing of the lower jaw, usually 5 times. The sound stems from the lower neck. It is a surprise or warning call which I label the 'something's up' call. A sound you would hear in the human realm if you were able to hear Julia Child stepping into a very cold shower.

The tremolo is the only sound uttered while in flight and also during "crippled wing" and "penguin dancing." In those activities it is more rapid with a strained, higher pitch.

The yodel is by far the most complex sound made and is said to only be made by the male. I question this, having one time observed a pair I felt sure were both making the sound at the same time. It is an aggressive call made during confrontations of any sort. It is obviously very taxing to utter, involving the whole body. I label it the "that's close enough" call. Sometimes it is compared to an angry seagull's call, although it is much more complex and threatening.

Loons need nearly 300 acres of open water for solitude during the reproductive season. Intruders, in the air or on the water, will be warned with the mighty male's yodel.

"*I assume the "coos & mews" that I have heard are variations and combinations of the hoot and wail. I've heard these during nesting, when pairs are exchanging chores. Also when close contact with very small chicks is involved. The sounds are very communicative and gentle.*

As the loons were only 10 feet from my blind, I could hear them as they conversed with coos, mews & moans. They were not hoots or wails...but seemingly a mixture of both of them. What a treat to be in on their intimate discussion and understand it!"

1994

The hoot is a simple, one-note sound. It is made by a quick contraction of the abdomen. It is a casual means of contact during calm periods. It is obviously a means of giving location without alarm. I have heard it in very dense fog and during the night. The latter was more prevalent on cloudy nights or nights with little or no moon. I label it the "are you there?" call. It varies greatly in pitch.

Without hearing the loons' call, it is impossible to understand them from a description, much less what the experience does to your senses. Sounds vary a lot, sometimes attributed to variations in individual birds. There are, too, uncategorized nuances acquired as these sounds are cried upon the reverberating currents in differing weather conditions of these Northern lakes. Whatever the case, the loon's resilient song is wonderfully refreshing to the human spirit.

"The loon's cry is a stamp upon the northern wilderness. Its sound upon the water is like a tree reaching for the sky, it's just the way it is; no one wonders why."

1994

Looning

"The Lord did well when He put the loon and his music into this lonesome land."

Aldo Leopold

June 15, 1924

"Today I have learned something new about loons nesting, all is not where and what we may think!"

1994

"*oday I watched loons in the stillness of early morning mist. My heart was warmed by the simple scene. Glistening droplets of chilled water ran from the silky feathers of the loon's head and neck down its back and on into the mirror-calm water. There is much to gain from such a morning but words elude me. This simplistic beauty of nature engenders warmth in my heart, such beauty I cannot recreate....*"

1994

109

"*My shooting was to no avail this morning. The blackflies and mosquitoes dominated my attention. Bug spray was of no use. My skin was covered but they went through my clothing and entered my jeans through some well-worn tears on each knee.*"

1994

For me it is hard to cast a "Westriver" or "44" over a weed bed for Northerns without looking about for natural offerings. As I reel the reflective spoon, more than once I've been guilty of losing concentration by the sound of a loon in the distance. I look about in vain, only to hear my lure jam up at the tip of the rod. Embarrassed, I then look around to see if anyone has noticed my ineptitude.

"*The cliffs on the north side of the Big Loge are a great lookout for loons. This seems to be a flyway of sorts. The view isn't bad either!*"

1994

"The sunrise was wonderful this morning. The silhouetted young family was a touching sight. The 2-day-old chick kept getting under the wing of one of the adults so getting the right shot took awhile."

1994

"*Oct. 1 - a.m. - 36° - foggy - loons in fog - loons w/color - In flight (coming in), loons & distant color, reflections, fog & sun, ducks & grebes - p.m. - Walking ferns, water & leaves, fall leaves & stream, reflections.*"

 127

1994

"*In the deafening silence of a cool Canadian night the utterances of the loon echo from the cool waters into the mountains and on up to the heavens. The air has literally come alive with wails, tremolos, and yodels that have become the dominant sound of this Northern wilderness. The gentle melodies of Song Sparrows, the piercing cries of a Sharp-shinned Hawk, and the chorus of burping bullfrogs and nervous insects seem only to add atmosphere to the interesting arias that ensue. Sounds pour constantly from the loon, being interrupted only by short intervals of silence and wavering chaos. It is not the sound of the maniacal or weird. It is a song of life and freedom, an unleashing of spirit that leaves an indelible mark on all who receive it.*"

1982

"*I can't help but feel that there ought to be aspects of their lives that are uniquely known only by loons themselves. Such a solitary creature of wildness needs a certain amount of mystery about it, at least for me. Loons need privacy and solitude. Sometimes they are very withdrawn, preferring to be heard and not seen.*"

1992

Photo Facts

All photographs included in this book were taken from 1982 through 1994. To ensure accuracy of habitat and inhabitants which surround the common loon, all photographs were taken in one area. They were all taken in the wild in natural conditions in natural light. No flash, filters or computer manipulation was used in any photos.

Equipment used is as follows:
Cameras - Nikon FE, F3 & F4S
Lenses - 400mm 3.5, 300mm 4.5, 105mm 2.8, 50mm 1.8 & 24mm 2.8
Tripods - Bogen 3221 & Slik U212
Miscellaneous - TC 14B (teleconverter) & PK 13 (extension tube)
Film - Kodak Lumiere 100x (LPZ), Fuji RVP 50 (Velvia) & Kodachrome 64 (K64)

Page#	Title	Lens	Exposure	Film	Date
1	Loon Calling	400 mm	1/500 @ f3.5	LPZ	June 1994
2-3	Loons at Sunset	105 mm	1/125 @ f4	Velvia	June 1994
4	Loon on Nest	400 mm	1/15 @ f3.5	Velvia	June 1994
8-9	Loon Calling	400 mm	1/250 @ f3.5	Velvia	August 1992
10	Pink Lady's Slipper Orchid	105 mm	1/8 @ f11	Velvia	July 1994
10	Loon & Young	400 mm	1/250 @ f4	LPZ	August 1992
11	Canadian Sunset	24 mm	1/2 @ f22	Velvia	August 1992
12	Loon & Fog	400 mm	1/1000 @ f5.6	Velvia	August 1992

Gavia immer

Page#	Title	Lens	Exposure	Film	Date
14-15	Loon Stretching	400 mm	1/500 @ f4	LPZ	June 1994
16	Loons at Sunset	400 mm	1/125 @ f3.5	Velvia	August 1992
18	Loon & Chicks	400 mm	1/250 @ f3.5	Velvia	August 1991
19	Loon Stretching	400 mm	1/250 @ f3.5	LPZ	July 1994
20	Loon Surfacing	400 mm	1/500 @ f3.5	LPZ	July 1994
20-21	Loon Diving	400 mm	1/500 @ f3.5	LPZ	August 1994
22	Loon Taking Off	400 mm	1/1000 @ f3.5	LPZ	August 1991
23	Loon in Flight	400 mm	1/1000 @ f3.5	LPZ	August 1992
23	Loon Taking Off	400 mm	1/1000 @ f8	LPZ	August 1992
24	Loon in Flight	400 mm	1/500 @ f3.5	Velvia	August 1992
25	Loons Gliding	400 mm	1/2000 @ f3.5	K64	August 1988
26	Loon Bachelors	400 mm	1/250 @ f3.5	Velvia	August 1992
27	Loons in Flight	400 mm	1/1000 @ f4	Velvia	August 1992
28	Loon Shaking	400 mm	1/250 @ f3.5	Velvia	August 1991
28	Loon Shaking	400 mm	1/1000 @ f3.5	Velvia	August 1994
29	Loon in Fall Flight	400 mm	1/90 @ f3.5	LPZ	October 1994
30	Loon Approaching	400 mm	1/1000 @ f5.6	Velvia	August 1992
31	Loon Landing	400 mm	1/250 @ f4	Velvia	August 1992
31	Loon Landing	400 mm	1/250 @ f4	Velvia	August 1992
32	Crippled Wing Act	300 mm	1/500 @ f4.5	K64	August 1983
33	Loon Protesting	400 mm	1/125 @ f3.5	K64	August 1992
34-35	Loon in Fog	300 mm	1/125 @ f4.5	K64	August 1982

Posterity

Page#	Title	Lens	Exposure	Film	Date
36-37	Loon on Nest	400 mm	1/125 @ f3.5	LPZ	July 1994
38	Loons Courting	400 mm & TC	1/250 @ f4.5	LPZ	May 1994
39	Loons Bill Dipping	400 mm & TC	1/500 @ f4.5	LPZ	May 1994
40	Loon Turning Eggs	400 mm & TC	1/250 @ f4.5	LPZ	June 1994
41	Loon on Nest	400 mm & TC	1/250 @ f4.5	LPZ	June 1994
42	Loons in Pollen	400 mm & TC	1/125 @ f4.5	LPZ	May 1994
43	Loon Chick	50 mm	1/60 @ f5.6	LPZ	July 1994
43	Loon Family	400 mm	1/250 @ f3.5	K64	August 1991

Page #	Title	Lens	Exposure	Film	Date
80	Deer in Water	400 mm	1/125 @ f3.5	Velvia	August 1991
81	Fawn Swimming	300 mm	1/250 @ f4.5	K64	August 1985
81	Water Snake	105 mm	1/60 @ f11	LPZ	June 1994
82	Pine's Reflection	400 mm	1/60 @ f5.6	Velvia	August 1992
83	Black Duck Preening	400 mm	1/30 @ f3.5	Velvia	August 1992
84	Great Blue Heron	400 mm	1/125 @ f3.5	LPZ	June 1994
85	Lily Pads & Reflections	105 mm	1/8 @ f22	Velvia	July 1991
87	Gulls at Sunset	400 mm	1/250 @ f5.6	LPZ	June 1994

Claim to Fame

Page #	Title	Lens	Exposure	Film	Date
88-89	Loon at Sunset	400 mm	1/1000 @ f5.6	LPZ	June 1994
90	Loon Stretching	400 mm	1/1000 @ f3.5	Velvia	June 1994
91	Loon Calling	400 mm	1/500 @ f3.5	Velvia	August 1991
92	Loon Wailing	400 mm	1/1000 @ f4	K64	August 1988
93	Loon Wailing	400 mm	1/500 @ f4	Velvia	June 1994
94-95	Loon & Young	400 mm	1/1000 @ f3.5	Velvia	August 1992
96	Loon Overhead	300 mm	1/1000 @ f4.5	K64	August 1983
96	Crippled Wing Act	300 mm	1/500 @ f5.6	K64	August 1983
97	Penguin Dancing	400 mm & TC	1/500 @ f4.5	LPZ	July 1994
98	Loon Yodeling	400 mm	1/250 @ f3.5	Velvia	August 1991
99	Herring Gull Calling	400 mm	1/2000 @ f3.5	LPZ	July 1994
99	Loon Yodeling	400 mm & TC	1/1000 @ f4.5	Velvia	July 1994
100	Loon at Sunset	400 mm & TC	1/1000 @ f4.5	Velvia	July 1994
101	Loon Family	400 mm	1/500 @ f3.5	LPZ	July 1991
102-103	Loons in Fog	400 mm	1/125 @ 3.5	LPZ	September 1994

Looning

Page #	Title	Lens	Exposure	Film	Date
104-105	Loons in Fog	400 mm & TC	1/125 @ f4.5	LPZ	June 1994
106	Loon on Nest	24 mm	4 sec. @ f22	LPZ	July 1994
107	Loon on Nest	105 mm	1/15 @ f8	LPZ	July 1994
108	Loon Neck Stretch	400 mm	1/500 @ f3.5	Velvia	May 1994
109	Loon Backlit	400 mm & TC	1/250 @ f4.5	LPZ	July 1994
110-111	Loons at Sunrise	400 mm & TC	1/250 @ F8	LPZ	June 1994
111	Loon	400 mm	1/1000 @ f4	Velvia	July 1994
112	Loons & Fall Color	400 mm	1/125 @ f3.5	LPZ	October 1994
113	Loons in Fog	400 mm	1/60 @ f3.5	K64	August 1992
114-115	Fall Color	24 mm	1/2 @ f22	LPZ	October 1994
115	Loon Swimming	400 mm	1/500 @ f3.5	Velvia	August 1992
116	Loons Taking Off	400 mm	1/500 @ f3.5	K64	August 1992
117	Loons in Fog	400 mm	1/125 @ f3.5	Velvia	August 1994
118	Loon Backlit	300 mm	1/250 @ f4.5	K64	August 1983
119	Loons in Mist	400 mm	1/30 @ f3.5	K64	August 1986
120	Bachelors	400 mm	1/60 @ f3.5	Velvia	August 1992
121	Loon in Flight	400 mm	1/250 @ f3.5	K64	August 1992
122	Loon with Young	400 mm	1/250 @ f3.5	Velvia	August 1991
123	Loons at Sunrise	400 mm	1/125 @ f3.5	LPZ	July 1994
124	Loon Taking Off	400 mm	1/1000 @ f3.5	LPZ	June 1994
125	Loon in Flight	400 mm	1/1000 @ f5.6	Velvia	August 1991
126	Fall Flight	400 mm	1/90 @ f3.5	LPZ	October 1994
127	Fall Immatures	400 mm	1/90 @ f3.5	LPZ	October 1994
128	Loon at Dusk	400 mm & TC	1/90 @ f4.5	LPZ	July 1994
129	Loon at Dusk	400 mm	1/60 @ f3.5	Velvia	August 1991
130	Loon Preening	400 mm	1/1000 @ f4	Velvia	June 1994
130	Loon Preening	400 mm	1/500 @ f4	LPZ	June 1994
131	Loon & Young	400 mm	1/250 @ f3.5	Velvia	August 1991
132	Loon Protesting	400 mm	1/250 @ f3.5	K64	August 1986
133	Bachelors	400 mm	1/250 @ f3.5	K64	August 1992
134	Loon Landing	400 mm	1/500 @ f3.5	K64	August 1992
134-135	Fall Flight	400 mm	1/60 @ f3.5	LPZ	September 1994
136-137	Loons at Dawn	400 mm	1/500 @ f5.6	Velvia	August 1994
139	Loon Calling	400 mm	1/250 @ f3.5	Velvia	August 1991
141	Loons at Sunrise	400 mm & TC	1/1000 @ 5.6	LPZ	July 1994
143	Loons at Dawn	400 mm	1/250 @ f3.5	Velvia	July 1994

Loon Protection Organizations

North American Loon Fund
6 Lily Pond Rd.
Gilford, New Hampshire 03246

Common Loon Protection Project
Maine Audubon Society
P.O. Box 6009
Falmouth, ME 04105-6009

Loon Preservation Committee
Audubon Society of New Hampshire
R.R. 4, Box 240E
Meredith, NH 03253

Loon Survey Project
Vermont Institute of Natural Science
Woodstock, VT 05091

Loon Project
Audubon Society of New York
Hollyhock Hollow Sanctuary
Rte. 2, Box 131
Selkirk, NY 12158

Oikos Research Foundation
Syracuse Univ. at Utica
Utica, NY 13502

Loon Lake Loon Association
P.O. Box 75
Loon Lake, WA 99148

Canadian Lakes Loon Survey
Long Point Bird Observatory
P.O. Box 160
Port Rowan, Ontario
Canada N0E 1M0

Michigan Loon Preservation Association
6011 West St.
Joseph Highway
Suite 403, P.O. Box 80527
Lansing, MI 48908

Loon Watch
Sigurd Olson Institute
Northland College
Ashland, WI 54806

Montana Loon Project
411 W. Bush
Libby, MT 59923

Alaska Loon Watch
Alaska Department of Fish & Game
333 Raspberry Rd.
Anchorage, AK 99518

Gatineau Fish & Game Club, Inc.
Box 550
Maniwaki, QC
CN, J9E 3K6

Minnesota Dept. Natural Resources
500 Lafayette Rd.
St. Paul, MN 55146

MA Div. Fish & Wildlife Field Headquarters
Rabbit Hill Rd.
Westboro, MA 01581

finale

"In wilderness exists a calming rhapsody. A comfort indeed is this music to the fisherman who anxiously retrieves his laboring lure and the lone explorer as he paddles along a grassy shoreline of a lost lake. In this great symphony the master composer has penned every note. His voice runs through His instruments as inspiration. Far be it from me to orchestrate the song.

Herein lies a poor attempt to capture this song. I so often desire to live within the melody, happy to become part of the chorus. The music's rousing resonance runs, vacillating, through my soul. It echoes as I search to enhance my life. It disturbs me to know how often I find myself in discomfort around people yet so at ease beside the loon in its wilderness home. It is here I feel a oneness with my Lord. The loon comes as a visitor from heaven reminding me of a better place, and I look forward to that day when the score will be complete. Looking towards the sky I wait expectantly, knowing I haven't said "I love you" quite enough.

As I hear the wail of the loon I, too, cry out, 'Where are you?' My spirit yearns for absolution from above; like wanting to sing but needing a song. I look out over the reflective waters and see the beauty of nature encompassing me and thank the Lord above for putting in wilderness, song."

June 1994

IN WILDERNESS
Song
Litany of the Common Loon

Other books by Mr. Kirkpatrick:

FIRST IMPRESSIONS (1983)
WHISTLING WINGS: The Beauty of Ducks in Flight (1989)
WILD MISSISSIPPI: A Natural View (1993)
THE NATURALIST'S JOURNAL: A Book for Records, Notes & Observations (1994)

For more information on prints, books & related materials contact:

Thy Marvelous Works
P.O. Box 31414
Jackson, MS 39286
(601) 362-7100